Red Wine for Your Health

Red Wine

FOR YOUR HEALTH

Andrea Schaffer

SARASOTA PRESS

U.S. and Canadian Cataloging-in-Publication Data available upon request.

ISBN: 1-55356-001-9

Published in the United States in 2001 by
Sarasota Press
an imprint of Key Porter Books Limited
4808 South Tamiami Trail
PMB #205
Sarasota, Florida
34231-4352

Published in Canada in 2001 by
Key Porter Books Limited
70 The Esplanade
Toronto, Ontario
Canada M5E 1R4

Originally published in German in 1998 by W. Ludwig Buchverlag GmbH for Verlaghaus Goethestrasse GmbH & Co. KG, Munich

www.keyporter.com

Translation: Elizabeth Schweiger
Design: Patricia Cavazzini
Electronic formatting: Jean Peters
Photography: Mir Lada, pp. 2, 7, 10, 30, 34, 35, 39, 43, 51, 54, 58, 70, 71, 75, 78, 79, 82, 83, 86, 90, 94; Image Networks Inc.: pp.14, Gary Conner; 38, Mark Gibson; 50, Matthew Borkowski; 62, Chuck Burggraf; 67, Inga Spence
Food and Prop Styling: Patricia Cavazzini

Printed and bound in Canada

01 02 03 04 05 6 5 4 3 2 1

Contents

CHAPTER 1

Red Wine—Yesterday and Today

Pleasure and Health

For thousands of years, wine has been enjoyed as a drink and also used for medicinal purposes.

No other man-made beverage is as ancient or as closely intertwined with the history of human civilization as wine. The Bible tells us that even in antiquity our ancestors knew how to extract grape juice and make wine. Since the days of Noah, wine has been a constant companion, across diverse cultures and epochs, occupying a unique place as a beverage that is appreciated for both its taste and its medicinal properties.

The central role of wine in people's lives even millennia ago is immediately apparent from the many references to it in the Bible. Wine is praised as an enjoyable and intoxicating substance that can take the edge off the harshness of life, and also lauded for its curative powers. The following sentence, attributed to Paul in a letter to Timothy, illustrates just how knowledgeable people were in biblical times with regard to the healing effects of wine:

"Abstain from drinking water and use some wine instead, for the benefit of your stomach and because you are often ill."

It is surely no coincidence that many a biblical miracle was performed with or in the presence of wine. One need only think of the Last Supper—a central ritual in Christian religion to this day—which is based on the transformation of Christ's blood into wine.

Wine in Antiquity

In ancient times, wine was appreciated for more than just its role in bacchanalian drinking sprees. Early physicians became increasingly aware of wine's curative powers. When medical science was still in its infancy, wine was rarely used undiluted. Instead, it was applied mostly to stabilize and preserve the pharmacological components in medicinal plants. It is likely that wine was also often added to improve the taste of bitter herb extracts. Thus, many recipes have been preserved from ancient China, Egypt and Greece in which wine is listed as a basic ingredient in the preparation of tonics derived from plants.

Through trial and error, the physicians of antiquity gradually began to trust in the healing power of wine. Hippocrates was the first to use undiluted wine to treat illness, in about 400 BC. He recommended it, among other uses, as a restorative agent, a nerve tonic and a sleeping draft, as well as a beverage to treat headaches and mood swings, for cardiovascular irregularities, and with problems involving eyesight or digestion. The disinfecting properties of alcohol or wine were also known; drinking water was mixed with small amounts of wine to improve its quality.

Hippocrates introduced
purified wine into the
repertoire of the healing
arts.

Recognizing the Curative Powers of Wine

There are also numerous documents indicating the therapeutic use of wine in other times and places. Recent experiments and research studies confirm that our ancestors did not overestimate the curative powers of fermented grape juice, and since the late 1970s attitudes towards moderate consumption of alcoholic beverages, especially red wine, have begun to change.

Moderate wine consumption is believed to protect against many ailments, above all heart disease, a major concern in Western industrialized nations, where, statistically, it is the leading cause of death. According to estimates, abnormal or pathological changes to the coronary vessels could decline by approximately 40 percent and the risk of cardiac arrest could be reduced by 10 to 20 percent if every adult were to drink one or two glasses of wine each day. The low rates of heart disease and heart attack in the traditional wine countries of the Mediterranean support this theory. Of course, other lifestyle habits are contributing factors to this disease, so typical of modern civilization. Overweight and a high-fat diet, too little exercise and excessive stress are considered to be the main risk factors for coronary heart disease.

The Current Wine Revolution

The advantages of regular, albeit moderate, wine consumption are also beginning to be recognized by national health authorities. Recently, the American government has added its voice to the worldwide scientific community: its latest official guide on

Nowadays the focus is on the preventive effects of red wine. It helps in the fight against diseases of the coronary vessels and heart attack.

nutrition includes a recommendation that daily, moderate consumption of wine may be beneficial to your health. One U.S. vintner has reportedly even been allowed to print "promotes good health" on his labels. Considering the neo-prohibition tendencies that are gaining momentum in the United States today, this recommendation would surely never have been allowed to pass without incontrovertible proof that moderate alcohol consumption is beneficial, especially in the case of red wine.

However, caution is advised: do not misinterpret the "pro-alcohol" messages of recent years. They are by no means intended as a license for uncontrolled drinking. On the contrary, excessive alcohol consumption continues to be a risk factor for many diseases. Recent research has simply taught us to look at the topic of "alcohol consumption" in a broader manner. Whether alcohol is ultimately healthy or unhealthy depends to a large degree on overall consumption and the choice of beverage. This book discusses why red wine in particular is good for one's health, especially when it is taken daily and in moderate amounts, and how, specifically, it promotes coronary health. The details are explained in the ensuing chapters.

CHAPTER 2

Cardiovascular Disease—

The Scourge of Our Time

In recent years, women have overtaken men as the group most at risk of dying from cardiovascular disease. It used to be the other way around.

Every year, there are more than one million heart attacks in the United States alone. But the toll is even higher: cardiovascular-related diseases claimed almost a million American lives in 1997—that is 41 percent of all deaths—making it the leading cause of death, even ahead of cancer, which led to a little more than half as many deaths.

The statistics are staggering. Some 60 million Americans suffer from some form of cardiovascular disease. Among the many cardiac disorders—heart insufficiency, heart attack, heart rhythm abnormalities (arrhythmia) and others—arteriosclerosis and the changes it causes in the blood vessels plays a particularly large role in many resulting diseases. These dreaded deposits are especially common in the arteries of the elderly. Among all people who die of cardiovascular disease in the United States each year, some 80 percent are over sixty-five years of age. However, one in three men and one in ten women can expect to develop a major cardiovascular disease *before their sixtieth birthday*. And 34 percent of deaths from cardiovascular disease are premature deaths, involving individuals who are below the average life expectancy.

For decades, cardiovascular diseases were associated primarily with men. However, this has changed dramatically in recent years. More women than men are now affected by cardiovascular problems in North America. Statistics gathered by the American Heart Association clearly confirm this trend: in 1997, 503,000 American women died of cardiovascular causes as compared with 450,000 men. In Canada, 36 percent of all male deaths in 1995 were due to cardiovascular disease, while it accounted for 39 percent of all female deaths.

There are two main reasons for this development. One is the increased life expectancy among women, and hence the higher risk of falling victim to cardiovascular disease. For a long time the risk of cardiovascular disease to women was underestimated because women tend to experience heart attacks ten to fifteen years later in life than men. As life expectancy increases, more women are living to an age where they fall victim to this disease.

The other important reason lies in changed lifestyles among women, more and more of whom are adopting habits and behaviors formerly associated with men, including such risk factors as stress and smoking, in addition to new patterns in professional life. Nevertheless, doctors and women themselves continue to underestimate the risk of heart attack for the female population.

Regardless of whether the person at risk is male or female, prevention is a high priority! In other words, only reducing or removing several of the known risk factors can help to prolong life and, in the long term, decrease health costs to society at large.

Prevention is the magic word, but it's easier said than done.

Each of us is aware that our life depends upon the smooth functioning of the heart, the pump that distributes blood throughout the body; and we know that the beginning and end of life are determined by the heart's activity. But we remain ignorant in many ways of the heart's functions, or at least we rarely pay attention to them, taking the ever-present heartbeat for granted.

And the heart carries out an enormous task! This hollow muscle, about the size of your fist, is a combined pressure and suction pump that permits blood to circulate continuously through the network of veins; this is the basis for keeping the body alive. Blood circulation nourishes every cell in your body, supplying oxygen via the arteries and then "extracting" it again via the venous cycle. The effort required to perform these tasks must not be underestimated.

> Lowering the cost of treatment remains a challenge to cash-strapped medical systems.

Costs at a Glance
Cardiovascular diseases pose a major challenge not only from a medical but also from an economic perspective. The direct costs for treating cardiovascular diseases and their symptoms are estimated at $26 billion in the United States per year. This represents one-third of the total expenditure for hospital care in the United States. If one adds the indirect costs to these figures—that is, the monies lost in sick days at work, unfitness to work and disability compensation—then the overall cost rises to approximately $325 billion per year. The Heart and Stroke Foundation of Canada puts the annual economic cost of cardiovascular diseases at $18 billion.

Moreover, this marvelous pump is capable of adapting in an amazing fashion to each situation and condition faced by its "owner." Regardless of whether he or she is sleeping or running, under stress or in love, the healthy heart continues to function and adapt for many years.

How Your Heart Works

To enable the heart to perform its duty, nature has designed it as a double pump comprising two heart chambers and two vestibules. The right chamber suctions "used" blood and pumps it into the lungs, where it is enriched with oxygen (a process called lesser pulmonary circulation). From the lungs, this "fresh" blood flows to the left heart chamber, whence it is pumped into the body (greater, or systemic, circulation). Each contraction of the heart muscle pumps the equivalent of approximately one cupful of blood through the system. The cardiac valves prevent blood from flowing back again.

The heart muscle is activated by, among other factors, hormonal and electrical stimuli from the brain, taking its energy from the nutrients in the blood transported directly to the heart through the network of coronary vessels. To guarantee the smooth functioning of the circulatory system, the heart performs sixty to eighty beats per minute on average; that is several hundred thousands per day and easily forty million heartbeats a year. In a person at the age of eighty, the heart muscles have contracted more than three billion times—without interruption!

The blood circulates through the body via a complex system

of vessels. The blood vessels are differentiated according to the task they fulfill:

- The **arteries** are responsible for transporting oxygen-enriched blood in the process of greater (or systemic) circulation. At the same time, oxygen-deficient blood flows through them from the right half of the heart to the lungs, where oxygen is absorbed and carbon dioxide is unloaded. The oxygen content in blood is visible to the naked eye: oxygen-rich blood is bright red. The walls of the arteries are quite thick and elastic, because these vessels need to be able to withstand the pressure from the heart pump.
- The **veins**, whose walls are thinner than those of the arteries, transport consumed and oxygen-deficient dark red blood back to the heart. They also return blood that has been enriched with oxygen in the lungs back to the left side of the heart, whence it is pumped throughout the entire body.
- The blood vessels get thinner and thinner the closer they are to the body surface, terminating in the fine vessels called **capillaries**. These vessels are so narrow that only single blood cells can pass through. The miniature vessels are extremely "porous" or permeable, thus ensuring that oxygen and nutrients can pass from the blood into the tissue and thence into every cell. At the same time, the capillary system is also where the exchange of metabolic products occurs: carbon dioxide is brought from the tissue into the blood, which is then transported to the venous bloodstream for processing.

To ensure that blood doesn't accumulate in the lower extremities, the heart must function simultaneously as a suction and pressure pump. The best way to support this function is through movement and exercise. Strange as this may sound, the heart has

Color is an indicator of the oxygen level in blood: bright red blood is rich in oxygen, while dark blood is oxygen-poor.

Factors That Make the Heart Work Harder

• When we eat a high-sodium diet, our body stores too much liquid. The volume of blood increases and the heart therefore has more to pump.

• Nicotine narrows the blood vessels and raises blood pressure. Moreover, the toxins in the "blue smoke" promote the thickening and hardening of the arterial walls (arteriosclerosis).

• A high-fat diet increases cholesterol levels in the blood. Cholesterol in turn can attach itself to the arterial walls and lead to arteriosclerotic deposits. The result: the arteries and blood vessels become narrower and blood flow is hindered.

• Pieces of plaque (the deposits in the walls of the arteries) can break off and get swept away in the bloodstream, thereby clogging smaller vessels over time. The situation becomes critical when a vessel or artery is completely blocked. If coronary vessels are affected, a heart attack ensues. When the same happens to cerebral vessels, the victim suffers a stroke.

• Similar life-threatening situations can occur when the clotting factor in the blood is unbalanced and the blood literally stops flowing. This may lead to thrombosis, or clot formation, and thus completely block a blood vessel, leading, in the most extreme case, to pulmonary thrombosis if a thrombus (blood clot) separates and becomes stuck in a lung.

• Deficient production of insulin, the hormone the body

secretes after meals to metabolize sugar, leads to high blood sugar levels, making the blood thicker. When blood sugar is unbalanced over a long period of time, that is, when diabetes goes untreated or is difficult to manage, direct damage to the small and large vessels may result.
• And last but not least: negative psychosocial stress—constant aggravation at work, unemployment, feelings of hopelessness, lack of fulfillment on an ongoing basis, or continual conflicts with a life partner, to name but a few examples—can be a definite risk factor.

to work less hard when we are walking at a moderate pace than when we are standing or sitting. Any additional effort by the heart takes its toll if the blood composition varies or the vessels are damaged. This is the danger posed by the risk factors that are discussed in greater detail later in this chapter (see page 27).

In general, advancing age is accompanied by a number of lesser or greater ailments, and the performance of all internal organs begins to deteriorate. Naturally, the heart too is affected by aging. Transfer errors in the conducting system lead to irregularities in the heart rhythm (arrhythmia); in other words, the heart loses track of its own beat. Infections and rheumatism can damage the cardiac valves, and sometimes even the entire heart muscle.

Since the pressure in the vascular system as a whole gradually declines with the passing years, the heart in its role as a pump organ must compensate for this weakening by working harder and harder to achieve the same effect. However, such age-related changes can usually be accommodated fairly easily as long as the heart isn't subject to any additional burdens. Possible triggers for these supplementary pressures on the heart are the risk factors mentioned later in this chapter with regard to arteriosclerosis (excessive stress, nicotine or alcohol, overweight, an unbalanced diet and lack of exercise). Yet high blood pressure and heart insufficiency have reasons for existing in the first place.

What is High Blood Pressure?

Blood pressure is the pressure present in the heart chambers (or ventricles) and in the vessels. It makes blood circulation possible in the first place. On the other hand, blood pressure is dependent on heart performance and on the elasticity and resistance in the blood vessels. The pressure with which blood is pumped through your body changes several times throughout the course of each day and night. These short-term fluctuations are perfectly normal, because blood pressure is influenced by many factors, such as posture, breathing, and physical and emotional exertion (stress); it also adapts to our sleeping or waking state. Generally speaking, the lowest blood pressure levels occur when we sleep and the highest when we are subject to extreme exertion.

Blood pressure becomes a concern only when it remains high even when we are at rest. High blood pressure is especially dangerous for the arteries, because they are then exposed to an even higher pumping pressure than usual. High blood pressure, called hypertension in medical terminology, therefore translates into a constant demand on the stability and elasticity of the arteries, a veritable "rupture test" for the arterial walls.

Approximately one in four North American adults suffers from high blood pressure! The problem is that half of these individuals with hypertension are unaware that they are at risk because there are generally no side effects or symptoms. This is a ticking time bomb because lack of treatment or inappropriate treatment for high blood pressure will, over time, lead to a dangerous level of stress on the blood vessels and the heart.

It is often difficult to determine the causes of hypertension with any certainty. In approximately 10 percent of all cases, the

SYSTOLIC

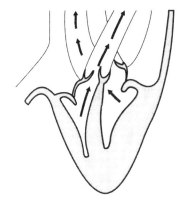

Contract and Pump

DYSTOLIC

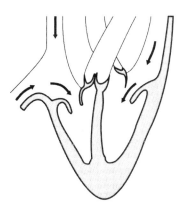

Relax and Refill

Blood Pressure—What is Normal?
In measuring blood pressure, there are two values to consider. The lower value indicates the diastolic phase, that is, when the heart slackens and is refilled with blood (See *Figure 2*). The higher value indicates the systolic phase, when the heart contracts and presses blood into the arteries (See *Figure 1*). Blood pressure is measured in mmHg (millimeters on the barometric column) and is abbreviated as RR in honor of the inventor of this measuring method, Dr. Riva Rocci.

In most adults, normal diastolic pressure is below 90 mmHg and systolic pressure is below 140 mmHG. Any values above these readings are considered to represent elevated blood pressure. Hypertension is present when the values are consistently above 95 mmHg diastolic and/or 160 mmHG systolic during repeated blood pressure readings.

Figures 1 and 2: Systolic and dystolic phases of blood pressure.

underlying cause is a hormonal imbalance, for example, or a kidney infection. In most cases hypertension is accompanied by other risk factors, which are mentioned in connection with arteriosclerosis (see page 27). In addition to a high-sodium and high-fat diet, these are tobacco consumption, lack of exercise, and stress. However, there is no conclusive evidence for a fundamental "trigger" of so-called essential hypertension. Rather, it tends to be the result of many accumulating factors.

What Causes Cardiac Insufficiency?

Cardiac insufficiency (myocardial hypofunction or weakness) occurs when the heart is no longer capable of pumping blood satisfactorily into the body's circulation system. In the early stages, hypofunction manifests itself in rapid fatigue and shortness of breath (for example, when climbing stairs); other symptoms include water retention, interrupted sleep and the avoidance of lying on the left side. Keeping in mind the different tasks performed by the two halves of the heart (see page 16), we differentiate between left and right myocardial hypofunction.

Again, several causes may come together to produce a weakness in the heart. One possibility is an abnormal enlargement of the heart muscle or poor oxygen supply to the heart cells. But hypertension that has gone untreated can also result in the heart muscle being chronically overburdened and thus lay the groundwork for heart insufficiency.

When is Heart Rhythm Disturbed?

The heart does not function automatically; it must be stimulated to do so. This is accomplished by means of electrical impulses, which are created by the heart itself and transmitted within the heart muscle to certain cells. These stimuli cause the heart to contract and thus pump blood through the body's circulatory system; in other words, the heart is beating.

If this stimulating function is somehow disturbed, for example as a result of a deficiency in important nutrients, or if the stimuli transmitters aren't functioning, then the normal heart rhythm can be interrupted. The heart will then beat either too slowly, too rapidly, or irregularly.

The heart contracts because it receives an electrical stimulus. If disturbances of the heart rhythm interfere with the organ's proper function, a pacemaker is often required to regulate the stimulus production.

Focus on Arteriosclerosis

Arteriosclerosis (or hardening of the arteries) is the name given to a change in the blood vessels that is in part localized and in part spread across a larger area. In contrast to a healthy blood vessel, an artery affected by arteriosclerosis no longer has a smooth, elastic inner surface; instead, the interior wall is rough, broken and irregular. If you could touch it with your bare finger, it would feel knobbly and rough in parts. In most cases the rough areas are deposits of lipids and other materials. These hardened areas develop over time into so-called plaques, which in turn contribute to the thickening of the arterial walls. This not only has a negative effect on the elasticity of the blood vessels, but it is accompanied by a decrease in the diameter of the blood vessel, which severely hinders blood flow.

Throughout the 1980s and 1990s intensive studies were undertaken to determine the causes of arteriosclerosis and to seek possible therapies and treatments. Hardly a year passed without new hypotheses being published and yet more items being added to the list of factors that cause arteriosclerosis. In recent years there have once again been new and interesting theories on how arteriosclerosis develops, and these will surely inspire and indeed necessitate a new approach to treatment.

Notwithstanding all our progress, however, the true origin of arteriosclerosis and the thickening of the arterial walls remains unclear. Experts continue to debate several hypotheses about premature vascular aging, each a possible explanation either on its own or in combination with one of the others. In this respect, doctors speak of risk factors as being primary or secondary (i.e., combining with others to aggravate an existing problem). See the box on page 27.

Arteriosclerosis: A Convergence of Many Risk Factors

Experts agree that one factor which contributes greatly to the development of arteriosclerosis is a raised level of cholesterol in the blood. When cholesterol levels are high over a prolonged period of time, biochemical chain reactions are triggered and the cholesterol is converted into sluggish foam (or xanthoma) cells. Together with dead cells, connective tissue and elastic fibers, these foam cells form the arteriosclerosis plaques, which narrow the affected vessel and ultimately block it completely. The result is a heart attack.

Sixty percent of the cholesterol needed for the organism's functioning is produced by the body itself; the remaining forty percent must be acquired from external sources. This explains why cholesterol levels can be regulated to such a large degree by diet.

Scientists hypothesize that in some cases arteriosclerosis begins with a deposit of the cells from a fresh blood clot in the interior arterial wall. If these thrombi—that is, the clots—aren't immediately located and dissolved, they can contribute to a thickening of the arterial walls, a change that may lead to arteriosclerosis.

A similar reaction occurs when the tissue is stressed as a result of a strong mechanical effort (such as is present in the case of high blood pressure). Arteriosclerosis-related changes are then the equivalent of the body's own repair work: the arterial walls are slightly injured as a result of the constant high pumping pressure, scar tissue forms, the walls thicken and the diameter of the vessel is decreased.

Homocysteine, an amino acid that is formed temporarily during internal cell reactions, has been identified as another possible risk factor caused by the metabolism. Although homocysteine is produced by the body itself, when concentrations are too high it can change and severely damage the arterial walls, thereby promoting arteriosclerotic deposits. Cell metabolism and thus the homocysteine level can be adversely affected above all by a deficiency in vitamin B, especially B6 and B12.

Another theory is that immune processes may be involved in changes to the vessels. According to this premise, a weakened immune system would contribute to the development of arteriosclerosis because "lame" immune cells would continue their battle against intruders such as viruses and bacteria for far too long, thereby creating a breeding ground for inflammations, which in turn damage the cells in the blood-vessel walls. Recent research results do in fact support the supposition that bacteria

Many interesting theories about the causes of arteriosclerosis and about possible new methods of treatment have been published in recent years. The only certainty, however, is that the disease does not present a uniform clinical profile.

trigger processes that lead to arteriosclerosis. However, this thesis continues to be controversial among cardiologists, and it will undoubtedly be some time before we are told to take antibiotics for arteriosclerosis.

One thing is certain: arteriosclerosis does not present a uniform profile. The common phrase in medicine is "a multi-factor course of disease." Diagnosis, assessment and treatment are therefore dependent upon the primary risk factors as well as the location of the plaques or vessel blockages.

The following triggers have been established as the main risk factors for arteriosclerosis in addition to predisposition (family history) and continuous stress: high blood pressure, heavy smoking, raised cholesterol, overweight, lack of exercise, diabetes mellitus, and specific illnesses that are linked to blood-clotting disorders and inflammation of the arterial walls. When several of these factors converge, the risk of developing arteriosclerosis is considerably higher, possibly even exponentially increased. The most vulnerable age group are people over sixty years old, with men and women being equally affected. Even a single factor, such as diabetes, can present a risk and so should be discussed with a doctor.

Effects of Arteriosclerosis

One of the main clinical reasons why a thickening in the arterial walls as a result of arteriosclerosis is a serious condition is that, generally speaking, the coronary and cerebral vessels are affected, as well as the peripheral vessels, which means that vital areas are put at risk. However, arteriosclerosis is a silent,

The Key Risk Factors for Arteriosclerosis

Primary risk factors
- High blood pressure
- Diabetes (diabetes mellitus)
- Metabolic disorder
- Smoking

Secondary risk factors
- Lack of exercise
- Overweight
- Stress

The risk of arteriosclerosis increases exponentially: when two primary risk factors converge, the overall risk increases fourfold, and in the case of three risk factors it can increase tenfold.

Arteriosclerosis is a silent disease. Deterioration of the vessels usually remains unnoticed until serious consequences occur.

and hence largely undetected, disease, until a thrombotic blood clot or arterial blockage occurs. Depending upon the site where the vessels are being obstructed, the profile of the disease can vary widely.

Coronary Heart Disease—An Overview

In many cases arteriosclerosis affects the coronary arteries. The most frequent cause is the strong pumping pressure that the blood vessels near the heart must withstand. This represents a permanent mechanical stress, which can lead to slight damage of the interior layer of the vessels and thus to circulation disorders, as mentioned earlier on. When the vessels in and around the heart itself are affected, we speak of coronary sclerosis.

Noticeable symptoms tend to occur only when the diameter of the arteries has been reduced by half and the flow of blood is correspondingly hindered. At that stage the entire heart muscle can no longer be supplied with sufficient blood and hence with sufficient oxygen. (See *Figure 3*, page 29) These symptoms are described in medical terms as typical coronary heart disease.

Angina Pectoris—A Constriction of the Chest

When the heart, already subject to poor blood supply as a result of arteriosclerotic narrowing in the vessels, is exposed to an additional stress—regardless of whether it is physical or emotional in nature—the balance between oxygen supply and oxygen requirement is compromised even further. A sudden difficulty in breathing is frequently the result, and this may progress to become angina pectoris. The symptoms of angina are sudden short-term pain beneath the sternum, which may radiate to the left shoulder and down the inside of the left arm. These sudden attacks may be accompanied by a crushing sensation of constriction in the chest and feelings of suffocation, which may lead the sufferer to believe that he or she is near death.

Myocardial Infarction—A Critical Lack of Supply

If a section of the plaque on an arterial wall breaks loose, or if a blood clot forms, there is a danger that one coronary artery may become completely blocked. This will most often occur in areas that are already narrowed as a result of arteriosclerosis. The blockage causes a sudden arrest in the oxygen supply to the tissue behind the artery. As a result, the cells in this area are usually

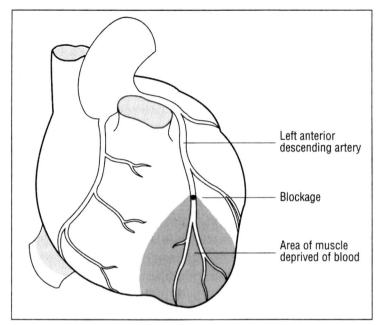

Left anterior
descending artery

Blockage

Area of muscle
deprived of blood

Figure 3: Diagram of a heart with arteriosclerosis.

severely damaged or even killed. Hence, a myocardial infarction
always results in a diminished capacity of the heart muscle (heart
insufficiency); in extreme cases myocardial infarction can be life-
threatening. According to estimates, more than half of all myocardial infarctions are fatal

Since a myocardial infarction always causes serious damage
to the heart tissue—in direct relation to the severity of the infarction—few patients recover fully, and reoccurrence of myocardial
infarction is therefore a major concern. From this point onwards,
at the very least, the patient must undergo a rigorous regime of
secondary prophylactic measures, avoid as many risk factors as
possible and usually take medical therapy.

Stroke—An Infarct in the Brain

When blood flow to the brain is partially interrupted because of an artery blocked as a result of embolism or thrombosis, or if an artery hardened by arteriosclerosis, and thus brittle and porous, ruptures in the cranium, the result is a stroke (apoplexy). Because various areas of the brain are shut down, a stroke is usually followed by some degree of paralysis and loss of speech.

Peripheral Arterial Obstruction

Obstructions in the branchlike peripheral arteries occur frequently in the extremities, most commonly in the legs. One familiar warning sign of these changes is the so-called "window-shopping disease," most common among diabetics and heavy smokers. Because of poor circulation in the leg muscles, the patient suffers severe pain after walking a short distance, which often forces him or her to stop and rest before being able to move on. It is the typical behavior of the patients that has given the disorder its curious name: the breaks in between walking are often camouflaged as window shopping. In cases of advanced or severe arterial obstruction, the affected foot or lower leg may have to be amputated.

Avoiding Risk Factors

The complications and symptoms described above can be pre-vented. Modern insight into the development of arteriosclerosis leaves no doubt that the changes to the vessels occur as a gradual process that is therefore controllable, above all through lifestyle. Exercise, non-smoking and a healthy diet are the primary pillars of prevention. The inclusion of wine in a healthy menu is becoming increasingly important in this context. The big surprise is that wine can reverse the impact of certain risk factors or even eliminate them.

We need only take a look at France, where culinary pleasures are an intrinsic part of the culture. Although animal fat figures relatively prominently in the typical French diet, mortality rates from heart attack or stroke are low. The reasons for this seeming paradox are explained in the next chapter.

Arteriosclerotic changes develop over time, allowing for positive intervention.

CHAPTER 3

The French Paradox

French cuisine is known for its variety and fine taste, but it does not conform to widely held beliefs about what composes a healthy and balanced diet.

We always think of the French when it comes to culinary know-how. To "dine in the French style" is the epitome of gracious living, for the French have always known how to make eating into an opulent pleasure, and nothing has changed in that respect. Be it a small rural establishment or a five-star restaurant in Paris, the delicacies on the plate are usually specialties of the house, or at least of the region.

Another common element of French dining is multiple courses. There are small appetizers to begin with—hors d'oeuvres like duck liver pâté or a piece of lamb in orange sauce—followed by the actual appetizer, an onion soup, tuna salad, or escargot with garlic butter. Pâtés, omelettes and sausage from Normandy also fit into this category. The main course—the culinary and visual highlight of every French meal—differs considerably from region to region. Along the Atlantic coast the preference is for mussels and fish; in Gascony the specialty is *cassoulet*, a casserole of pork, garlic sausage, beans, tomato paste and herbs; the Loire region is renowned for its *matelote d'anguille* (eel ragout); and the famous Provençal fish soup, *bouillabaisse*, is served in and around Marseilles. The fourth course is usually cheese, an item never missing from a complete menu. Then, the French usually indulge their sweet tooth with *crème caramel, mousse au chocolat* or *tarte tatin* (apple tart), to name but a few frequent favorites. And to top it all off there is an espresso, a digestive drink, and a cigarette or cigar. *Vive la France!*

Now, any health-conscious reader will protest that juicy pâtés, truffles and thick sauces—these ingredients so admired in French cuisine—surely have nothing to do with good nutrition. This diet is too fatty; a French person consumes approximately one-third more fat than the average American. As well, there are too many carbohydrates and too few vitamins, trace elements and ballast materials. And last but not least, nicotine consumption is still frighteningly high in France. Yet despite all these "unhealthy" diet and lifestyle habits, France is one of the countries with the lowest rates of heart attack and stroke (see table on page 36). What is the explanation for this apparent contradiction, which has come to be described as the French paradox?

The first scientist to discuss this phenomenon publicly, thus drawing worldwide attention to it, was Professor Serge Renaud. Renaud worked at INSERM (Institut National de Santé et Recherches Médicales). In his work he analyzed a number of statistical findings which showed that France had one of the lowest rates of cardiovascular disease in the entire world. "As a middle-aged American, your risk of dying of a heart attack is three times as high as that of a Frenchman of the same age. Therefore, the French are doing something right, which the Americans are doing wrong," said Renaud. When asked what this might be, he answered, "It's simple: the answer is alcohol." While the French and Italians have the highest wine consumption in the world (up to eight ounces of wine, usually red, per day), wine consumption is very low in the

Scientists recognized as early as the 1980s that moderate consumption of red wine can lower the risk of heart attack.

United States. In other words, despite a high-fat diet, relatively high nicotine consumption and a lack of regular exercise among the French population as a whole, red wine, or rather the beneficial ingredients it contains (see chapter "Red Wine—No Ordinary Beverage"), provides such effective protection for the coronary vessels that heart attacks are relatively rare.

The French scientist Renaud was not alone in regarding moderate, long-term wine consumption as an effective prophylactic measure against cardiovascular disease. As early as the 1980s, Dr. Arthur Klatsky, a renowned cardiologist from California, had reached the same conclusion after studying 129,000 patients. Wine drinkers (in contrast to beer drinkers), Klatsky said, ran a markedly lower risk of suffering myocardial infarction. And in 1991, Sir Richard Doll, an internationally renowned expert on epidemiology and now professor emeritus at Oxford University, made the following statement at a conference of cardiologists in Sydney, Australia: "I believe the scientific findings should be interpreted that men and women who drink alcohol regularly, but moderately, are not only less likely to suffer or even die from heart disease, but that their overall mortality with regard to all causes of death is better than in those who abstain from alcohol."

Differences in Myocardial Infarction

Let's return to the so-called French paradox. At first, Professor Renaud's theory was criticized by many of his scientific colleagues. While the low rate of heart disease in France had been a known fact for some time, certain of the statistics had been gathered in erroneous fashion, and critics felt that Renaud's conclusions

The known risk factors do not explain the differences in heart attack rates between countries.

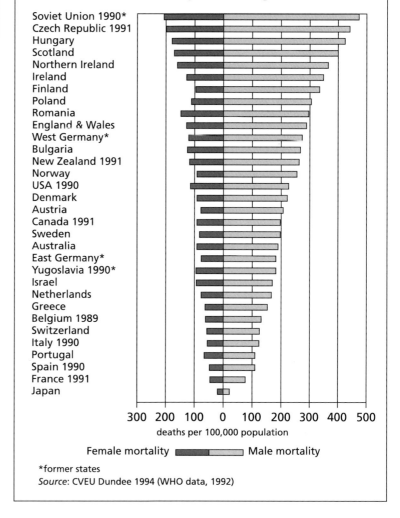

Heart Disease
Mortality in Men and Women ranging from 40 to 60 years of age

Soviet Union 1990*
Czech Republic 1991
Hungary
Scotland
Northern Ireland
Ireland
Finland
Poland
Romania
England & Wales
West Germany*
Bulgaria
New Zealand 1991
Norway
USA 1990
Denmark
Austria
Canada 1991
Sweden
Australia
East Germany*
Yugoslavia 1990*
Israel
Netherlands
Greece
Belgium 1989
Switzerland
Italy 1990
Portugal
Spain 1990
France 1991
Japan

300 200 100 0 100 200 300 400 500
deaths per 100,000 population

Female mortality   Male mortality

*former states
Source: CVEU Dundee 1994 (WHO data, 1992)

therefore stood on weak foundations. For example, one could not discount the possibility that the causes of death given in the statistics may have reflected country-specific "medical currents." At the beginning of the twentieth century, for example, it was common practice in the United States to list the cause of death as an undiagnosed heart disease in cases where no other specific cause was identifiable. However, these too are but vague speculations, assumptions and musings.

The heated discussion of this phenomenon has gone on at great length without leading to a conclusive result. One thing is clear, though: many doctors and scientists are ultimately baffled when it comes to the true causes of the development of cardiovascular disease. It is true that a list of risk factors has been clearly identified: smoking, high blood pressure and elevated cholesterol levels to mention but the most common. Nevertheless, these factors alone are not satisfactory in explaining why the statistics on heart disease differ so dramatically between, say, France and the United States or England, for example.

For this reason a series of studies was conducted in the latter half of the 1980s and early 1990s focusing on the etiology of heart disease. In 1985 the World Health Organization (WHO) commissioned a long-term study, which became known among experts as the MONICA study. For this project, data on thousands of patients who had suffered a heart attack were gathered and statistically analyzed in forty-one cities worldwide. In contrast to earlier studies, care was taken to record the cases according to uniform parameters in order to make comparisons possible. The result, presented after ten years of MONICA by a British research team headed by professor Dr. Hugh Tunstall-Pedoe, was impressive indeed.

Comprehensive studies confirm the French paradox: the rate of heart attack among the French is remarkably low, despite the fact that their diet is high in fat.

The number of heart attacks among men in Toulouse, in southern France, was a mere 240 per 100,000; in Lille (France) the figure was 314 and in Strasbourg (France) 336. In other southern regions the statistics were either comparably favorable or even better, as in Vaud/Fribourg (Switzerland), which recorded 253 per 100,000. By contrast, the figures from northern Europe were shocking: Glasgow had 823 heart attacks per 100,000 inhabitants, Belfast 781. The North American statistics fell between these two extremes. In other words, the French really do have a very low risk of cardiovascular disease—as low, in fact, as other southerners. Yet in contrast to their Italian and Spanish neighbors, whose typical diet is fairly low in fat, the French consume a great deal of unsaturated fat.

Etiological Research of a Phenomenon

The French paradox had been proven. Yet the reasons underlying this nutritional phenomenon continued to provoke heated debates. Professor Renaud, who had now gained unexpected popularity, believed that the facts were there for all to see. In an article published in the prominent scientific journal *The Lancet* he wrote: "One might be surprised at the high alcohol consumption and low mortality rate in Toulouse. But these observations only confirm earlier reports according to which wine consumption and fatal heart disease in industrial

states have been shown to be related, and where the possible positive effect of alcohol can mostly be traced back to the consumption of wine."

Under closer scrutiny, this explanation proved unsatisfactory on its own, and Professor Renaud himself doesn't link the French paradox only to the regular wine consumption of his compatriots; he is convinced that their diet is not nearly as bad as it may appear at first glance. The French love fresh fruit and vegetables, as well as cheese and other milk products, which are staples of French cuisine, and all of these foods fall into the "healthy" category. Moreover, in France meals are a leisurely affair, enjoyed in a relaxed atmosphere and with many breaks between courses, giving the metabolism ample time to extract nutrients and digest food. Still, Renaud insists that of all factors influencing cardiovascular health, wine is the most important. For example, a comparison of cholesterol levels between men in Toulouse and men in Glasgow will show few differences, as will a comparison of systolic blood pressure. Cigarette consumption too—a known risk factor in the development of cardiovascular disease—is barely less in France than in England or Scotland. The only major difference between these populations lies in wine consumption, where the French are miles (or perhaps we should say liters) ahead of the English and of North Americans and northern Europeans as a whole.

It is important here to draw attention to another research project, the Copenhagen City Heart Study. This study, commissioned by the Danish Ministry of Health, the results of which were published in the spring of 1995, became the focus of an American television documentary. The panel comprised Dr. Morten Gronbaek, director of the Copenhagen City Heart Study, Professor Curt Ellison, a doctor and epidemiologist at Boston University, and our old friend Professor Serge Renaud from Lyon. Each expressed the same opinion: daily consumption of wine lowers mortality rates from cardiovascular disease, by nearly 60 percent according to this study.

This was the big breakthrough! The documentary made huge waves in the United States, and over the following days wine stores in the U.S. and Canada racked up unprecedented sales. People were buying red wine of all kinds, and within four weeks wine merchants' profits rose by 45 to 50 percent. The trend has continued to this day.

In Europe too, the good news about the beneficial effect of wine consumption spread like wildfire. Many doctors felt vindicated, since wine had been regarded as a medicinal as well as pleasurable beverage in Europe for centuries.

The following chapters provide insight into why wine is so beneficial for coronary health and discuss the results of further scientific studies on wine.

What You Should Know about Alcohol Consumption

Two Sides of the Same Coin: Use and Abuse

> Excessive consumption of alcohol continues to be a serious risk factor for ill health. However, in moderation, alcohol can be quite beneficial.

The news that red wine, an alcoholic beverage, should be hailed as the ultimate preventive against heart disease provoked consternation and, understandably, a skeptical reaction in medical circles. Wasn't it alcohol whose excessive consumption led to heart disease, heart attack and stroke in the first place, not to mention its many other tragic consequences?

Although few doubts remain today as regards the beneficial effects of moderate alcohol consumption, a nagging doubt persists about this newly discovered "heart medication." It is easy to understand that doctors who are confronted day in and day out with the consequences of alcoholism may feel uncomfortable encouraging their patients to drink alcohol, even though there may be plenty of medical research to support this recommendation.

What is more difficult to understand is why there remains some official public resistance to alcohol consumption of any kind, which makes no distinction between use and abuse. What the discussion around alcohol needs is nothing more than an unprejudiced and intelligent presentation of the facts. On pages 56 to 73 you will learn about the ingredients that mark red wine as a "gentler alcohol" and about those substances in red wine that help to protect the heart.

The Secret Lies in the Volume

The complication when discussing alcohol arises from its dual character, as both a simple drink to accompany food and also a potential intoxicant with considerable risks to one's health. There is no question that the same rule that applies to medication also applies to alcohol consumption: the dosage must be healthy! In small doses, alcohol is beneficial to mental well-being and physical health, and it also helps to create a relaxed atmosphere, which can facilitate communication and human interaction.

Abuse is another story altogether. Here illness, addiction and social isolation are the result. The risks of alcohol abuse are well known and are mentioned here only as an aside, because they are not the subject of this book. However, one cannot stress often enough that excessive consumption of alcoholic beverages cannot be condoned and that it does not lead to the health benefits described in the following paragraphs, which derive from *moderate* alcohol consumption only.

More is Not Better

Regular consumption of large amounts of alcohol poses a serious threat to the human body on a number of levels. These are the most common consequences of alcohol abuse:

• cirrhosis of the liver, which can lead to liver coma and death if untreated
• chronic inflammation of the pancreas, also life-threatening
• pathogenic changes to the heart muscle and thus diminished heart performance
• cancer in the oral cavity, throat, larynx, esophagus and liver; in women, also risk of breast cancer
• high blood pressure and thus a higher risk of heart attack and spontaneous cerebral hemorrhage, leading to stroke
• changes to the nervous system and mental state

The first positive scientific news about alcohol came as early as 1926.

Abstinence and Longevity?

Although the medical community has only recently begun to apply scientific methods to the study of the relationship between alcohol and health, the knowledge that drinking some alcohol can be beneficial to one's health is by no means new. American biologist Raymond Pearl had many positive statements to make with regard to alcohol as early as 1926. He found that people who drank moderately lived longer than teetotalers; excessive drinking, however, went hand in hand with a correspondingly steep

Mortality risks are lower for light to moderate alcohol consumers than for abstainers. This advantage diminishes proportionate to increased consumption, indicating that too much alcohol sharply increases the risk of death. This explains the U- or J-shaped mortality graph.

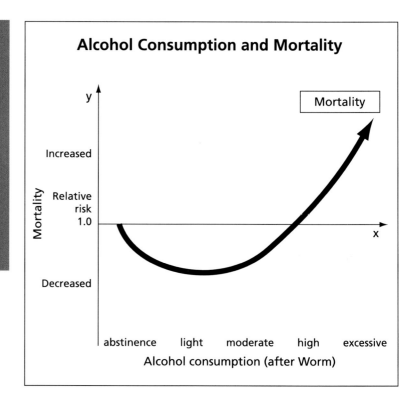

Alcohol Consumption and Mortality

rise in mortality risks. Pearl drew the famous U- or J-shaped curve, which is used to this day, to illustrate the relationship between alcohol consumption and mortality rates.

This correlation has been confirmed in a total of twenty-nine long-term studies on over one million people, observed for periods of up to nineteen years. The decisive element was that the increased mortality among teetotalers was not rendered invalid because the group might include former alcoholics; the same results were reached when the latter group was left out altogether. This proved once and for all that the mortality curve was not (as skeptics had assumed) driven higher by the inclusion of former heavy drinkers whose health was already compromised by their excessive alcohol consumption in previous years.

How Does the U or J Mortality Curve Emerge?

Alcohol consumption is indicated on the x-axis and mortality rates on the y-axis to create a graph that illustrates the relationship between these factors. If the mortality rate is set at 1.0 for teetotalers, then the mortality rate for the consumer of alcohol can be shown as a "relative risk" in relation to that of teetotalers. The curve clearly demonstrates that even very low alcohol consumption has a positive effect on the mortality rate (the relative risk drops to below 1.0). The risk is lowest when alcohol consumption is light to moderate; here, mortality rates are 40 percent less than those for teetotalers. Only when consumption rises above moderate is the relative risk the same as that of teetotalers. This creates the U-shaped mortality curve. As alcohol consumption increases further above moderate, the relative risk far surpasses that of the non-drinker and rises steeply; the curve begins to resemble a capital J.

Alcohol—a Health Tonic?

Since the early 1970s, the health benefits of moderate alcohol consumption have been the subject of systematic research. The results from more than sixty independent, large-scale, highly controlled and carefully analyzed studies from different countries around the world yield the following summary:

> The contention that moderate alcohol consumption is beneficial to your health when compared with complete abstinence has now been confirmed in more than sixty studies.

> **Various investigations agree that alcohol consumption can raise general life expectancy.**

Moderate drinkers are much less frequently the victims of coronary disease, suffer fewer strokes and have an overall lower pathogenic mortality rate than teetotalers. Excessive alcohol consumption, on the other hand, has always been and continues to be a major risk factor for many health problems—a truth that we should take to heart. Conclusion: moderate drinkers have the highest life expectancy. (What is meant by "moderate" consumption is explained in detail in "How Much Wine is Good?" on page 83.)

The Wider Health Benefits of Alcohol

It has been proven that the benefits of alcohol go beyond the prevention of cardiovascular disorders. Moderately taken, alcohol inhibits the production of gall and bladder stones. It also lowers the risk of falling prey to non-insulin-dependent diabetes mellitus by lowering blood sugar levels. And last but not least, moderate alcohol consumption can improve brain function in old age.

Having said that, even the many positive findings about alcohol consumption in recent years have not been able to prove conclusively that there is a causal link between moderate alcohol consumption and longevity. It is impossible to prove such a link one hundred percent, no matter how convincing and scientifically and methodically correct the studies may be; too many factors influence health and thus life expectancy to allow the isolation of any single parameter, in this case alcohol. Nevertheless, scientists feel that a basic relationship is highly plausible. The arguments that support this supposition are:

- the remarkable consistency in the results of all studies;
- the correspondence in results for men and women, from

different population groups in different areas of the world, and across different age groups; and

• the dose-dependent impact of alcohol, documented in countless experiments, on various body systems, for example metabolism and blood circulation.

Alcohol and Cardiovascular Disease

Of the many ways in which alcohol can influence health, it is the prophylactic effect on a healthy heart that interests researchers the most. Could it be possible that the "demon alcohol," of all things, may turn out to be an effective preventive against cardiovascular disease, the scourge of our time?

For more than twenty years, scientists around the world have been trying to get to the bottom of the link between moderate alcohol consumption and a healthy heart. This work began in the early 1970s with American physician Dr. Arthur Klatsky. Taking his patient card files as a basis, Klatsky gathered lists of risk factors and protective factors for heart disease. To begin with, he limited the data to 1,000 patients (500 with and 500 without heart troubles), but over the course of several years he expanded the research group first to 85,000, then to 124,000 and finally to 129,000. The result was consistently the same: moderate alcohol consumption protects against heart disease.

A 1976 study of 7,705 Japanese men in Honolulu reached the same conclusion. In addition to prevention of heart disease, the study also indicated a preventive effect against cancer and against stroke triggered by embolism. An Australian study in 1982 identified non-smokers who take alcohol moderately as the group with the lowest heart attack rates.

> Alcohol consumed in moderation protects above all against cardiovascular disease. This can be concluded from a multitude of population studies.

49

In 1986 the intermediate result of a cardiac study carried out on 2,100 men and 2,600 women in Framingham, Massachusetts, confirmed after an observation period of twenty-four years the U-shaped relation between alcohol consumption and mortality (see "How Does the U or J Mortality Curve Emerge?", p. 47). Subjects whose alcohol consumption was low were at the least risk of suffering a heart attack. This long-term study is still underway.

Another positive message about alcohol consumption resulted from an extensive study carried out in 1990 by the American Cancer Society. A study of 277,000 male subjects showed that one alcoholic beverage per day reduced the risk of cardiovascular disease by 25 percent and that moderate drinkers were less likely to get cancer than were teetotalers.

The result of a New Zealand study published in 1992 caused quite a stir. Comparative studies of patients who had suffered a heart attack and healthy subjects of the same age group indicated that the risk of heart attack was at its lowest twenty-four hours after alcohol consumption. It is interesting to note that the twenty-four-hour heart protection factor seemed to be particularly evident in women. The unequivocal finding that alcohol provided immediate as well as long-term heart protection was a sensation. Until then, the opinion had been that alcohol offered a kind of overall, underlying protection against cardiovascular disease, but that alcohol could, in the hours immediately following consumption, cause arrhythmia or even a heart attack.

We know that the risk of heart attack is lowered when alcohol is consumed regularly and in modest amounts. The same seems to apply to certain types of stroke.

Alcohol and the Risk of Stroke

Since the same faulty mechanism lies behind heart attacks and certain types of stroke, namely the blockage of a vessel as a result of a blood clot or plaque that has come loose, it is natural to investigate whether moderate alcohol consumption also protects against stroke. This link is more difficult to establish because stroke has many different causes.

In the case of ischemia (a reduction of blood supply to the brain) caused by thrombosis in a cerebral vessel, alcohol may play a preventive role because of its clot-inhibiting effect.

A completely different profile emerges in the case of stroke caused by hemorrhage resulting from a burst blood vessel in the brain. This form of stroke is often linked to chronic alcohol abuse. Indeed, many alcoholics die from the after-effects of a spontaneous cerebral hemorrhage, in which bleeding is prolonged because of high alcohol levels in the blood. It is obvious why alcoholics are especially

> Alcohol has a positive effect on the fat metabolism and in particular on the cholesterol level. The risk of arteriosclerosis declines proportionately.

prone to this kind of "burst pipe" in the brain: excessive alcohol consumption raises the blood pressure and thus the burden placed on the vascular system. How a rupture can easily happen in an already damaged area has already been discussed (see page 20).

With regular yet moderate consumption, however, the preventive effect of alcohol against the formation of blood clots surely outweighs any possible negative factors. At any rate, it seems clear that abstinence goes hand in hand with a higher risk of stroke than does moderate alcohol consumption, as has been documented in several studies on stroke.

More Protection for the Vessels

Research in recent years has documented that alcohol taken in moderation has more positive effects than harmful ones on the heart and the blood vessels. We must ask what the reasons are. Why does moderate drinking protect against cardiovascular disease, heart attack and possibly stroke?

It is well known today that alcohol provides protection for a healthy heart in several ways. The beneficial effect results largely from wine's impact on the metabolism: it increases the level of "good" (HDL) cholesterol in the blood, thereby counteracting unhealthy levels of fat in the blood and excessive cholesterol deposits in the arteries—a primary cause of arteriosclerosis and heart attack.

Cholesterol and Cardiac Health

Cholesterol is non-dissoluble in the blood and must therefore always attach itself to transport molecules in order to move

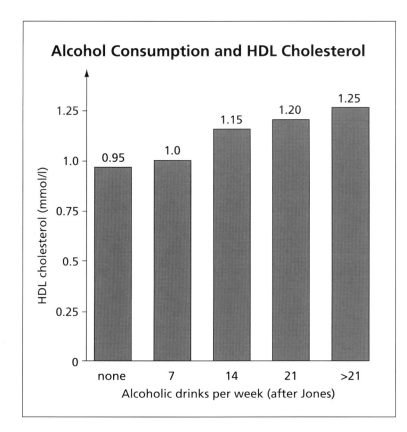

Alcohol Consumption and HDL Cholesterol

HDL cholesterol (mmol/l)

0.95 1.0 1.15 1.20 1.25

1.25
1.0
0.75
0.5
0.25
0

none   7   14   21   >21

Alcoholic drinks per week (after Jones)

Alcohol diminishes the risk of blood clotting in the coronary arteries. Thus, it provides secondary protection against the dreaded cardiac infarction.

through the bloodstream. These fat and protein formations, called lipoproteins, are differentiated according to size and density. Two groups of lipoproteins play an important role in cardiac health:

• Low-Density Lipoproteins, or LDL, are responsible for transporting cholesterol from the site of production, the liver, to individual cells. This group of lipoproteins is especially implicated in the development of arteriosclerosis and is therefore often referred to as "bad" cholesterol.

• High-Density Lipoproteins, or HDL, absorb excess cholesterol from the cells and transport it to the liver for catabolism (breaking down). The HDL group regulates cholesterol levels and is therefore often referred to as "good" cholesterol.

What matters in evaluating cholesterol levels in the blood is the balance between HDL and LDL cholesterol. High LDL levels in the blood are poison for the arteries. Over time these particles penetrate the artery walls and form deposits, which increasingly impede the free flow of blood; arteriosclerosis is the result. HDL works in the opposite manner. Therefore, high HDL levels in the blood are considered to be a good preventive against arteriosclerosis.

The positive effect of alcohol on HDL cholesterol levels and thus on the total fat metabolism, however, seems to be neither the only nor the most important protective factor. Greater importance is attached today to the fact that alcohol improves the flow and clotting properties of blood. In particular this means that the adherence of blood platelets (thrombocytes) is decreased; thrombocytes play a key role in the formation of blood clots in the coronary vessels and thus in causing heart attacks. Alcohol also decreases the concentration of fibrinogen, an integral component of blood clots, and moreover promotes fibrinolysis, the dissolution of existing blood clots.

Finally, scientists agree that two other effects of alcohol may play a role in promoting cardiac health: alcohol lowers stress, a major risk factor, and promotes blood flow because of its relaxing effect on blood vessels.

The above findings apply to all alcoholic beverages. Wine, beer or spirits—all can help protect against cardiovascular disease or

Cholesterol: Friend and Foe

High cholesterol levels are a major contributor to the development of arteriosclerosis. Although most health publications focus on the harmful effect of cholesterol, this lipid (fatty substance) is nonetheless essential, being required, for example, in the production of hormones, bile acid and vitamin D3, and in the regeneration of cell membranes. Without cholesterol the metabolic processes would fail. What matters is that cholesterol levels should not be high or elevated for any length of time.

Here is a general rule of thumb: An overall cholesterol level of less than 200 mg/dl is fine. When cholesterol levels rise to 250 mg/dl, the risk of heart attack is doubled, and at 300 mg/dl it is quadrupled. In addition to these absolute values, the ratio between harmful LDL cholesterol and protective HDL cholesterol is also vitally important. As a quotient of overall cholesterol, the following applies: HDL cholesterol below 4.0 is considered good, while a value above 4.5 is a cause for concern.

heart attack, always with the caveat that they must be taken in moderation. However, over the last twenty years evidence has been accumulating—and it is supported by the "French paradox" (page 32)—that red wine is far superior to all other alcoholic beverages when it comes to providing benefits for a healthy heart. The background story on red wine as the "gentler alcohol" is contained in the next chapter.

CHAPTER 5

Red Wine—No Ordinary Beverage

No Two Types of Alcohol are the Same

All alcoholic beverages can protect a healthy heart provided they are used appropriately and in moderation. Red wine, however, contains additional protective substances.

The information in the previous chapters on the relationship between alcohol and the development of various illnesses refers to all sources of alcohol, without differentiation. This oversimplification does not do full justice to the reality, especially since alcohol is usually not taken in its pure form, but as spirits, beer or wine.

Recently, science has tried to take into account the fact that most people develop a preference for a particular type of alcoholic beverage. While early studies focused on alcohol consumption in a general way, newer studies break the information down for beer, wine and spirits. Although comparative studies failed to yield wholly consistent results, they do demonstrate a clear advantage for wine, especially red wine, over other beverages. Taken regularly and in moderation, wine promotes a healthy heart in the opinion of many scientists, based on several different factors, and it also poses fewer risks than does a comparable consumption of beer or spirits. While moderate beer drinkers enjoy some health benefits, an equivalent consumption of alcohol in the form of spirits seems to pose certain health risks.

High Wine Consumption = Low Heart Attack Rates

The first hint of the advantages of moderate wine consumption was delivered in a 1979 study from Wales. Dr. Selwyn St. Leger, a passionate statistician, compared figures on heart attack rates from eighteen different industrialized countries according to beer, wine and hard liquor consumption in each country. The result of this comparison: low heart attack rates were always accompanied by high wine consumption, while no significant positive or protective effect could be detected for beer or hard liquor.

Caution!

Although many studies have observed a preventive effect for daily wine consumption of up to 20 ounces (0.6 l), this amount should not be regarded as a recommended guideline or entice anyone to increase their alcohol consumption. How much alcohol an individual can tolerate and how much alcohol is beneficial to health differs greatly from one person to another; it depends upon many factors, among them gender, overall fitness, climate and physical condition. For more details on this topic and a definition of "drink," turn to the section entitled "How Much Wine is Good?" on page 83.

Throughout the 1980s, study followed study, and all gave wine drinkers a better bill of health with regard to heart attacks than teetotalers, beer drinkers or hard liquor drinkers. In 1991, the work of Professor Serge Renaud received worldwide attention with his study of what has become known as the "French paradox" (see page 32).

In the mid-1990s, Professor Michael Criqui, epidemiologist at the University of San Diego, California, took a fresh look at the calculations previously carried out by his Welsh colleague St. Leger. Criqui's work was based on newer and more exact data for more countries, and it was analyzed with better, more elaborate calculation methods. His study, published in the highly respected journal *The Lancet*, confirmed the findings from the late 1970s: there is indeed a worldwide correlation between wine consumption and heart attack rates.

A similar outcome was produced in the same year by a statistical analysis undertaken at a research institute in Scotland. In addition, the scientists reached the conclusion that regional differences in the rate of heart attack could be better explained by looking at average wine consumption and vitamin E intake than by evaluating the fat content in the diet. Animal fat especially is considered a major risk factor for cardiovascular disease.

Do Wine Drinkers Live Healthier Lives?

The most remarkable development to date in the study of wine and health was probably the publication of the Copenhagen City Heart Study, led by Dr. Morton Gronbaek and published in the spring of 1995. In this long-term study, the alcohol consumption

Population studies established the beneficial effect of drinking moderate amounts of wine. Wine drinkers suffer fewer heart attacks compared with non-drinkers or consumers of beer or spirits.

The Copenhagen study shows a correlation between wine consumption and an overall mortality rate lower than that which accompanies abstinence or the consumption of beer or spirits. Compared with abstinence, beer shows no effect, whereas the consumption of larger amounts of spirits increases mortality rates.

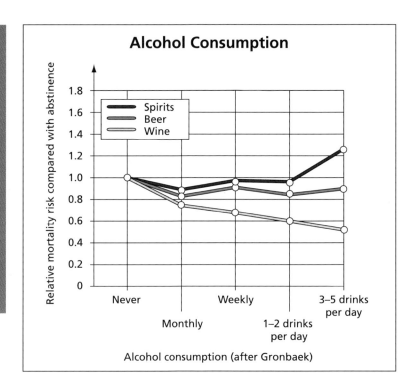

Alcohol Consumption

Alcohol consumption (after Gronbaek)

of 7,234 women and 6,051 men was observed for a period of twelve years and analyzed in terms of mortality among the same group. The result: wine drinkers had the lowest risk of dying from any type of heart disease, as well as the lowest mortality rate overall. Regular wine consumption was shown to produce increasing benefits up to a daily dose of three to five drinks. Anyone consuming three to five glasses of wine per day (the equivalent of 14 to 20 ounces or 0.4 to 0.6 liters) ran a 60 percent lower risk of heart attack than teetotalers and a 50 percent lower mortality rate overall. In contrast, the regular consumption of equivalent amounts of beer had no impact on mortality, while spirits—again calculated to equivalent volumes of alcohol—even raised mortality rates in comparison with the abstinence group.

The advantage enjoyed by wine drinkers compared with the other groups could not be explained by excluding other risk factors, such as lack of exercise, nor through criteria such as social standing, education level or income. Since the Copenhagen City Study is the only large study to date that has analyzed the effect of alcohol consumption according to the categories of wine, beer and spirits (carefully adjusting the amount in each case to compare the corresponding equivalent volume of alcohol), one can safely describe it as a milestone in wine research.

In the interest of fairness, it is important to note at this point that not all research groups have found wine to be superior in terms of promoting cardiac health. Although some health benefits were recorded in most studies of wine consumption, there have been contradictory findings. Some studies, for example,

The Copenhagen study showed not only a lower risk of cardiac infarction but also an overall increased life expectancy. The results of this study, with its careful design and thorough methodology, are greatly respected by other experts and often cited.

How Much Alcohol Does Wine Contain?
Everyone has seen the standard information on labels (for example: 13% alc./vol.), but few people understand what it really means in terms of alcohol content.

In beverages, alcohol content is measured as a percentage of total liquid volume. If a wine is labeled as having 13% alc./vol., then this wine contains 13 percent of its total volume as pure alcohol. So, a 40-ounce bottle of this wine would contain 5.2 ounces of alcohol; a 750 ml bottle would have 97.5 ml of alcohol.

were unable to show conclusively any preventive effect against heart attack for any of the beverages under investigation; other studies resulted in identical findings for wine and beer; and one study even reached the conclusion that the consumption of schnapps had a prophylactic effect. Therefore, many scientists are unwilling to state that drinking wine may have a preventive effect against cardiovascular disease.

Supporters of the "wine hypothesis" counter with the argument that most studies on this topic are riddled with methodological errors. For example, none of the studies—with the exception of the Copenhagen Study—compared the consumption of equivalent volumes of alcohol in wine, beer or spirits. Yet even the Copenhagen City Study, no matter how impressive, does not claim to deliver the ultimate proof of the beneficial effects of wine.

Nevertheless, a multitude of factors supports the plausibility of the results. The matching results of most studies are confirmed in laboratory findings: causative research as well as animal testing have shown that wine contains a number of substances in addition to alcohol that provoke a physiological reaction in the organism. Some of these substances are now being discussed as protective factors against cardiovascular and other diseases.

A young German scientist specializing in sports medicine, Professor Dr. Klaus Jung from Mainz, was able to prove the positive influence of wine, including white wine, on a number of blood factors in 1997. This chapter will inform you about these newly discovered "wonder weapons" in wine, and especially red wine.

Forces Hidden in Wine

Wine is an extremely complex liquid, consisting mostly of water, various types of alcohol, sugars, acids, tannic agents, proteins, vitamins, minerals and trace elements. Thus far, over one thousand ingredients have been identified in fermented grape juice. Which of these make wine into such a unique prophylactic against cardiovascular disease and other disorders is only gradually emerging.

Wine as a Source of Micronutrients

Micronutrient is a general term for the vitamins, minerals and trace elements required by a living organism. Of the vitamins, wine contains only a few from the B group and vitamin C in significant amounts. However, wine is rich in minerals and trace elements that are essential for a number of physiological processes.

> **The most important ingredients in wine are the phenols. These substances are also found in fresh fruits and vegetables, but in greater concentration in red wine.**

In particular, daily requirements of potassium, magnesium, iron, copper and manganese can be largely met through regular enjoyment of wine. Experiments have shown that several components in wine have a pharmacological effect, that is, an impact on metabolic processes.

The substances that are of most interest to wine researchers are the polyphenols. This group of plant substances is found in many fruits and vegetables and, to some degree, in the juices of both. In grapes, the valuable bioactive substances are contained above all in the skin, pits and stems, with amounts changing depending upon the type of grape, area of cultivation and degree of ripeness. Grape berries utilize their phenols as a kind of immune system to defend against parasites and fungi, and also for repairing bruises or cuts to the skin of the grape.

During the fermentation process, the phenols are separated out from the pits, skin and stems of the grapes. Ultimately, however, phenol content in any particular wine is dependent upon the ripeness of the grapes and the method of production. There are great differences between white and red wine. Since the phenol-containing grape skin is removed right at the beginning of the fermentation process in making white wine, it contains only one-tenth of the phenols found in red wine. In red wine production, the skin is left mixed in with the fermentation mass for a longer period of time, allowing for a richer phenol mix to develop. Still, phenol content can differ substantially between one red wine and another, not least of all as a result of rationalized processes in mass production. Generally speaking, wines that originate from small, traditional vineyards boast higher phenol content than mass-produced wines.

Cell Protection with Phenols

Why are wine researchers so fascinated by phenols? As we now know, some of the phenols in wine belong to the group called flavonoids. These protective materials are considered to be potent antioxidants—substances that protect the body from aggressive oxygen compounds called free radicals. The chemical structure of free radicals is characterized by a non-paired electron, which makes them highly prone to reaction. Unfortunately, in their search for a partner, the molecules also attack healthy cells. This process is called oxidation, and it leads to dangerous chain reactions that can severely damage the cell membranes and even the hereditary material. Phenol compounds offer free radicals the extra electron they are missing, thereby catching them and rendering them harmless.

The more care is taken in the making of wine, the greater the retention of phenols.

Flavonoids—Incidence and Importance

Plant pigments are called flavonoids. The name "flavonoid" derives from the Latin *flavus*, which means yellow, although they also produce the red, blue and purple coloring in fruits and vegetables. They have manifold effects on the organism. Flavonoids have antioxidant, anti-inflammatory and anti-allergenic properties, among others. They are sometimes also called vitamin P.

Red wine offers a uniquely broad range of flavonoids. These substances give wine its distinctive taste and character and are interesting from a medical perspective as effective antioxidants.

The Taming of "Bad" Cholesterol

In recent years, several studies have demonstrated the excellent protective function of antioxidants even for damaged coronary

Antioxidants—Protection against Free Radicals

According to the latest research findings, free radicals are responsible for the development of many diseases, especially cancer and cardiovascular disease, and are likely also involved in the aging process. Oxidation processes, and oxygen radicals in general, shouldn't be labeled as evil, however. From immunology research we know that these reaction-friendly molecules are part of the body's own anti-microbial equipment for our antibodies. Our bodies are in fact already equipped with enzymes that are responsible for "disarming" aggressive oxygen compounds. Only when the number of free radicals becomes excessive—as a result of various environmental toxins, radioactive radiation, infections and, above all, cigarette smoke—do the body's own protective mechanisms prove insufficient, permitting oxygen radicals to pursue their campaign of destruction without resistance. Once the balance between free radicals and antibodies gets out of hand, the body must resort to using antioxidants from nutrition. These strengthen the protective shield against the aggressive radicals by catching and immobilizing them. This is why antioxidants are also described as "radical catchers."

Phenols and flavonoids contained in red wine are not the only radical catchers known to us. Among the most familiar are vitamins C and E (which has become known for its beneficial effect on rheumatism and as a cell protection vitamin), as well as beta carotene.

vessels. How this curative power works has now been proven in laboratory tests.

The cholesterol issue was discussed earlier at some length (see page 52). What hasn't been mentioned is that LDL cholesterol isn't intrinsically harmful; rather, it is turned into an "artery killer" through the process of oxidation. Oxidized LDL compounds are dangerous and aggressive particles, capable of penetrating and injuring the soft artery walls. And cholesterol deposits in the arteries are the precursor to arteriosclerosis, which often ends in a heart attack. These processes can be slowed if the body is supplied with a sufficient number of antioxidants—for example, in the form of wine flavonoids.

Red Wine—An Antioxidant Powerhouse

Since nearly every vegetable and fruit contains vitamins and flavonoids, you may wonder why red wine in particular is recommended as a source of antioxidants. There are two reasons: first, the antioxidant compounds in red wine are more concentrated than in fruits and vegetables; second, flavonoids are stabilized by virtue of the alcohol content in wine. In fruits and vegetables—no matter how fresh—these valuable plant substances are partially lost during storage, transport and food preparation. The same applies to grape juice which, like all juices, contains surprisingly few flavonoids; it seems that it is the stabilizing effect of alcohol in wine that makes the difference. Just two glasses of red wine boost a person's natural intake of flavonoids by 40 percent.

We have already mentioned how laboratory tests have demonstrated that wine flavonoids inhibit LDL oxidation. Recent studies in this area show that the substances are absorbed in the gastrointestinal tract, whence they enter the bloodstream. The details of their effect are still unexplained.

First indications that flavonoids in wine really do inhibit or stop LDL cholesterol oxidation emerged in a test carried out in 1994. Japanese scientists published the results of a study on ten male test subjects who regularly drank vodka for two weeks and then wine for two weeks. Blood analyses showed that LDL oxidation was unaffected by vodka consumption but was strongly inhibited by wine consumption. This finding is yet more proof that all alcoholic beverages are not equal, an idea that is becoming more and more defined since the discovery of the "French paradox."

Red Wine—The Gentler Alcohol

A multitude of population studies have shown that drinking wine is accompanied by several protective factors and at the same time entails fewer risks than a comparable consumption of beer or spirits. Red wine owes its reputation as the gentler alcohol largely to the antioxidants it contains. While alcohol, a cell toxin, always leads to the formation of harmful free radicals—and this applies to wine as well as to any form of alcohol—red wine simultaneously delivers an antidote: the flavonoids, which destroy oxygen radicals by offering themselves as coupling partners. Thus, red wine compensates to some degree for the negative effects of the alcohol it contains. Testifying to alcohol's potentially damaging qualities is the marked diminishment in the body's supply of vitamin E—a potent free radical catcher—after the consumption of alcohol. However, this effect has not been observed after moderate consumption of red wine, because it simultaneously delivers sufficient amounts of antioxidants. White wine too can deliver a compensatory effect, albeit a less pronounced one.

Red wine contains over a hundred flavonoids. They aren't all antioxidants, and even among those that are, there are differences in terms of degree and potency. Currently, intensive clinical studies are underway to determine which red wine flavonoids are most effective in providing protection against heart disease. The flavonoids resveratrol, quercetin, catechin and epicatechin are most closely associated with the "wine miracle."

> Resveratrol is most abundant in wines from humid and cool regions.

The Wine Flavonoids

Resveratrol—Full of Promise

Resveratrol has emerged as one of the most interesting flavonoids in red wine. Resveratrol is a natural active agent contained in the wine grape. It combats fungal infestation, which occurs most frequently in the grape skin. It is logical that resveratrol is most common in grapes grown in moist and cool regions; fungal infestations have an ideal environment in such climate conditions, and therefore the plant's defenses must be particularly strong. Tests to determine the resveratrol content in various types of wine have shown that red wines contain fifty to one hundred times more of this protective substance than white wines. Within red wines, the content fluctuates according to the type of grape, its origin and the processing methods. In general, wines produced

The flavonoid resveratrol improves the cholesterol profile and counteracts blood clotting.

in humid and cool regions are richer in resveratrol than those from sunny and arid regions.

Although resveratrol was discovered in Europe and the United States only in the 1980s, it was by no means an unknown entity: in traditional Eastern medicine, the beneficial qualities of resveratrol have been utilized for hundreds of years.

Resveratrol in Eastern Healing

In China and Japan, people have been aware of the healing power of this plant substance for centuries. As the main ingredient of a medication called *kojo-kon*, resveratrol has been prescribed for arteriosclerosis and inflammatory illnesses, and more recently for fungus infections on the feet. In Asian traditional medicine, however, resveratrol was not obtained from grape skins but from the pulverized root of the healing plant *Polygonum cuspidatum*.

Recent research on resveratrol, initially carried out only in Asia but since the early 1980s also pursued in Europe and the United States, has confirmed the ancient knowledge from the Far East. Resveratrol has been proven to possess many pharmacological properties, all playing a protective role in terms of cardiovascular disease. In this regard it has been demonstrated that resveratrol as an antioxidant not only inhibits the oxidation of harmful LDL cholesterol (see page 53) but also effectively increases the concentration of the "good" HDL cholesterol. Moreover, this plant substance is able to weaken the coagulating properties of blood and thus inhibit the formation of blood clots, as well as counteract the production of inflammatory substances along the inner walls of the arteries.

Quercetin—An Unusual Career

Quercetin is abundant in nature, present in nearly all fruits and vegetables but especially in bulbous plants like garlic, onions and leeks. Red wine too contains pharmacologically significant amounts of this flavonoid.

Unlike resveratrol, which thrives in cool and humid regions, quercetin loves the sun. Hence the quercetin content in any individual wine is first and foremost determined by the amount of sun exposure. Once again, modern methods of mass production drastically reduce the presence of this valuable ingredient. However, nothing can interfere with its longevity; a hardy substance, quercetin retains its potency even after twenty or thirty years, in contrast to resveratrol, which weakens as the wine ages.

Since it was first discovered by science in the late 1970s, quercetin has had a remarkable career. It initially failed the standard Aimes Test, and was thereby branded as a carcinogen. Scientists were baffled, however, since it was already known that quercetin is a very common natural substance. Then the good news came in: the original test result had been adversely affected by a foreign substance introduced in the laboratory. Since then, this flavonoid has even been shown to be anti-carcinogenic, especially in cases of gastric tumors.

It is still unclear how the anti-tumor effect occurs. However, a picture is gradually emerging of the link between this flavonoid and cardiovascular disease. Quercetin, whose active form is absorbed into the circulation through the intestine, has been shown to prevent clumping of blood platelets and thus clotting. The hypothesis is that this effect, combined with its antioxidant

> **Quercetin is highly valued in medicine for its antioxidant and anti-inflammatory effect.**

properties, could play an important role in preventing heart attack and stroke.

Catechin and Epicatechin—The Great Helpers

The flavonoids catechin and epicatechin, which feature in relatively high concentrations in red wine, are remarkable for their powerful antioxidant effect. While epicatechin also displays anti-tumor properties, catechin has the additional benefit of decreasing the clotting tendencies of blood (thus helping to prevent stroke).

More than the Sum of Its Parts

The foregoing sections outline where current scientific knowledge stands with regard to wine phenols or flavonoids. Although much research remains to be done to decipher the ultimate secrets of red wine, one thing has already been proven: it isn't any single phenol component that makes red wine—taken regularly but moderately—into such an excellent preventive against cardiovascular disease, heart attack and stroke. Since the individual plant substances in wine do not duplicate one another's effect, the protective properties undoubtedly result from the various ingredients working together, as a team, to guard your health. The familiar adage of the total being more than the sum of its parts has never been more true. Whether the many laboratory results will replicate themselves in the human organism is a question whose answer is eagerly awaited. But the excellent statistics on cardiac health in France and other wine nations already seem to speak in red wine's favor.

No Rebound Effect after Drinking Wine

The consumption of alcoholic beverages is known to produce a rebound effect, a reaction that is in opposition to the initial effect. This means that several hours after drinking alcohol, when the clotting tendency is temporarily reduced, it then increases again quite considerably. Therefore, the risk of heart attack is especially high after an evening of partying and drinking. Alcohol-dependent oxidation processes are thought to be responsible for this rebound effect.

However, when red wine is consumed in quantities that contain an equivalent amount of alcohol as other drinks, there is no evidence of such a rebound effect. White wines seem to exhibit a similar benefit, albeit far less pronounced than in red wines.

> The protective effect on the heart is undoubtedly not attributable to any single component in wine. Instead, the combination of several flavonoids is most likely the decisive factor.

CHAPTER 6

More Benefits of Wine

In the past, people used wine to prevent intestinal infections. Proof of the disinfecting properties of wine has been provided by modern research.

Thus far we have discussed the relationship between wine and health predominantly from the perspective of cardiac health. In addition to this major theme, which is currently the focus of scientific inquiry, another aspect of wine should not be overlooked, one that was already well known to our ancestors in antiquity: the curative power of wine on the intestinal tract.

No Chance for Intestinal Pathogens

In ancient Greece, a small glass of wine, often mixed with water, was part of the daily diet across all levels of society. There were good reasons why wine was consumed not only for its taste but also as a component of regular nutrition: experience had shown that this strategy was miraculous in its prevention of stomach aches and diarrhea.

In the late nineteenth century, Parisians discovered that wine could even save lives. A cholera epidemic had broken out and those who drank wine were often spared from the dangerous intestinal infection. Many years later, a scientific experiment delivered proof that certain ingredients in wine truly are capable

of killing off cholera bacteria. In the experiment, red wine, white wine, wine diluted with water and pure water were each polluted with a specific amount of cholera bacteria. The bacteria survived only in the container of pure water; even in the diluted wine the micro-organisms soon perished.

Wine Prevents Travel Diarrhea

Travelers should take advantage of the well-documented and medically proven disinfecting and digestive properties of wine. Especially in warmer climates, tourists are often exposed to the risk of an intestinal infection from unsanitary conditions, polluted water and unfamiliar food. Taking a small glass of wine with every meal can effectively prevent the unpleasantness of travel diarrhea.

An American study explored this curative effect of wine. In a series of experiments, a wide range of diarrhea pathogens were tested for their resistance to vermouth—generally regarded as a good preventive for diarrhea—pure alcohol, tequila, white wine and red wine. The result: wine, especially white wine, even when diluted with water, is the best prophylactic against intestinal infections. While vermouth, which is often used for medicinal purposes, showed fairly good results, pure alcohol and tequila were virtually useless in fighting the bacteria.

Phenols (see page 64), which are extracted from grape skins during the fermentation process, are thought to be responsible for the disinfecting properties of wine. However, no explanation has been found thus far for white wine's superiority over red wine in preventing diarrhea.

Good for the Digestion

Folk wisdom has always said that the stomach and intestines can perform at their best only when the digestive juices are flowing. Today we can give the scientific reasons that underlie the ancient knowledge of wine as an aid to good digestion. Wine promotes the production of digestive secretions, thereby assisting the process of splitting the food we ingest into its smaller components and nutrients in the stomach and intestines.

As soon as wine reaches the stomach, it stimulates the glands in the mucous lining to release stomach acid. In addition, the alcohol contained in wine extracts gastrin from the stomach cells; this hormone is required for the production of protein-splitting enzymes in the stomach fluid. And finally, wine also ensures that the food mash in the stomach is well mixed, by stimulating blood circulation and hence the ability of the stomach muscles to contract.

When there is insufficient acid in the stomach, drinking some acidic wine with a meal can help to stimulate digestion. The beneficial effect of wine is the result of its acid components, whose potency is comparable to the stomach juices. Older people especially, whose digestion tends to slow down quite frequently, should take advantage of the balancing effect of wine on the acid in the stomach.

The liver and pancreas also benefit from a glass of wine taken with meals. Wine stimulates production of secretin, a hormone, which in turn stimulates the production of digestive juices in these organs. The pancreas especially, which is in charge of producing seven different enzymes, profits from the support provided

> Wine promotes the production of stomach juices, thereby making meals more easily digestible.

by wine; and with the pancreas performing well, the entire digestive system gets a boost. The secretions of this vital gland are needed for digestion in the small intestine. There, food is broken down into its smallest components, which are then transported forward into the body's circulation through the mucous membrane of the intestine.

To sum up: wine supports and stimulates all the essential steps in the digestive process, thus making an important contribution to all-round good health.

Lowering the Risk of Kidney Stones

The risk of developing kidney stones increases with age; with a diet high in calcium, potassium and animal protein; and with certain medications. Patients with a tendency towards kidney stones are usually asked to make sure they drink plenty of liquids.

As a recent study has shown, not all beverages are equally effective in preventing the formation of kidney stones. Wine was far ahead in first place, followed by beer, tea and coffee. Milk, water, orange juice and soft drinks with or without caffeine had no noticeable impact on the development of kidney stones. Grapefruit and apple juice, on the other hand, were shown to increase the risk of kidney stones.

As mentioned previously, alcohol in general is thought to help prevent the formation of kidney stones. While science has yet to explain why wine has the greatest prophylactic effect among all alcoholic beverages, the results of the above study can serve as another argument in favor of moderate and regular wine consumption.

Wine supports renal function and, more than other beverages (including beer), helps to prevent the formation of kidney stones.

CHAPTER 7

Practical Information about Wine

Everyone must decide individually whether or not to drink red wine. It is always helpful to consult one's doctor.

Most of the information in the preceding chapters has been from a theoretic and scientific perspective; in this chapter we will focus on the practical side. For example, what specific recommendations for consumption can we derive from the recent research findings with regard to alcohol in general and red wine in particular, and what is the correct way in which to use wine?

Wine is Not a Medication

First and foremost: red wine as a doctor's prescription—in other words, the sanction of the medical community for the use of wine as a specific medical prophylactic against cardiovascular disease—will surely never happen, regardless of the many "pro-alcohol" developments in recent years. The fear of contributing to alcohol abuse in society at large through such a recommendation is too great, and saving people from the risk of heart disease by increasing their risk of mortality from alcohol abuse is hardly the answer. Therefore, it must remain for each individual to decide for or against red wine. The following pages provide medical guidelines for appropriate wine consumption.

Enjoying Wine

There is another important thing to note at this point: despite the advantages it may offer, drinking wine is not compulsory for achieving good cardiac health. There are other simple options for supporting and promoting cardiovascular health—sufficient exercise and a good diet above all. If you don't like wine or cannot drink alcohol for whatever reason, you should leave it at that. It makes little sense to drink wine purely for "medicinal" purposes. After all, that would be completely counterproductive to the enjoyment and general sense of well-being that go hand in hand with drinking a good glass of wine.

Naturally, red wine is taboo for anyone whose medical

> **A "Drink" in the Language of Science**
> In science it is common to indicate alcohol doses by the number of "drinks." One drink corresponds to the volume commonly served in one alcoholic beverage (about 3½ ounces/100 ml of wine and 1 cup/250 ml of beer). According to the definition, one drink contains roughly 10 to 12 grams of pure alcohol. Light alcohol consumption, in medical terms, means a daily intake of one or two drinks, while moderate consumption averages three or four drinks per day.

condition precludes drinking alcohol of any kind; the same applies to recovered alcoholics. But even in these cases, people can still benefit from the healthy ingredients in red wine through dietary supplements extracted from red wine. This red wine in capsule form delivers all the benefits without the alcohol (see page 94 for further details).

However, anyone who is not restricted by health or other reasons, who enjoys a glass of wine and is confidently in control of his or her alcohol consumption should regard moderate enjoyment of wine as a health benefit.

How Much Wine is Good?

The first question that arises whenever we discuss the relationship between wine and health is this: how many glasses of red wine taken on a regular basis bring the desired benefits for cardiovascular health while simultaneously avoiding any concerns about excessive alcohol consumption? In other words, what precisely is the much-vaunted "moderate" consumption in concrete terms?

This question is not easy to answer. Various studies on the subject have produced recommendations ranging from one to five "drinks" for optimal benefits. ("Drink" in this context denotes not the type of beverage but a defined measure of alcohol. See the box on page 81 for a definition of "drink.") Furthermore, consumption even within this range of one to five drinks brings varying results. What this means is that determining the best approach to wine consumption for maximum health benefits is a true balancing act. While the properties that protect the vascular system are most effective at the top of this range—that is, with four or five drinks—this is the very same range at which the risk of falling prey to diseases caused by alcohol begins to increase.

Hence, scientific findings alone cannot help us to determine a concrete recommendation for practical use. Firstly, the definitions of both "drink" and "moderate" are fairly imprecise. And secondly, one can never assume that general guidelines for "moderate" alcohol consumption apply to each person equally. Individual alcohol tolerance depends on many factors, including gender, weight and predisposition. Depending upon an individual's own history or heredity, it may well turn into a balancing act poised between benefit and risk. In very general terms, women tolerate less alcohol than men.

Especially in cases of chronic high blood pressure, alcohol consumption of any kind always carries a risk, because blood pressure begins to increase after the second drink. The higher the daily intake climbs above this amount, the greater the risk of disorders caused by high blood pressure or other alcohol-induced effects. Eventually, the risks will outweigh the benefits for the heart and vascular system. When we consider how common high blood pressure is in today's society and, moreover, how often it goes undetected, ticking away like a time bomb while the victim remains unaware of it, the more we should pay attention to these concerns.

Only a doctor's assessment can fully ascertain for each person whether moderate alcohol consumption will bring benefits or pose risks. Age, gender, past experiences with alcohol, family history, and the overall risk of heart attack, certain types of cancer and other diseases must all be taken into account.

Alcohol Consumption and Women

According to today's scientific knowledge, one to three glasses of wine a day can do no harm. However, one must consider gender-specific differences: men can allow themselves one to three glasses of red wine per day (about 1¼ cups/300 ml), while no more than 3½ ounces (100 ml), or one glass, is recommended for women. There are good reasons why women should be more restrained in their alcohol consumption than men. To begin with, most women have less body mass and a smaller volume of blood than men; in addition, women lack an enzyme that is present in men and ensures rapid metabolic breakdown of alcohol in the system. The result is that women's blood alcohol levels become elevated much more quickly than men's.

Scientific studies also suggest that more than one drink per day may increase the risk of breast cancer in women. There are some studies on this topic that have found no correlation between wine consumption and breast cancer, identifying beer and spirits as the dangerous beverages. However, any family history of breast cancer should be taken as an indication to treat alcohol consumption of any kind with great care.

When Does Alcohol Pose a Risk to Women?
A sweeping study at Harvard University has shown that consumption of up to 29.9 grams of alcohol (contained in

approximately 1¼ cups/300 ml of wine) considerably lowers women's overall mortality rate compared with women who abstain, and especially the cardiovascular mortality rates. Women over fifty and those who already presented some risk factors for heart attack benefitted the most from the ingredients in wine known to protect the heart. Wine produced markedly better results than beer or spirits. On the other hand, the Harvard study also documented that when daily intake went above 15 grams, incidences of breast cancer and cirrhosis of the liver increased. Therefore, women should not exceed one or two drinks per day without a careful benefit–risk analysis. When daily consumption is higher than 30 grams, the overall risk of mortality increases by comparison with abstinence, with cirrhosis of the liver and cancer being the leading causes of death.

Naturally, alcohol consumption should be strictly avoided during pregnancy and breast-feeding.

In Moderation with Meals...

For most wine drinkers it is natural to enjoy the fine grape regularly but in moderation. This is largely due to the fact that wine—unlike other alcoholic beverages—is usually served with a meal, which automatically places certain limits on its consumption.

Aside from the advantage of curbing intake, it is generally best to take any kind of alcohol with meals and not in between. On the one hand it helps the digestion and on the other hand the alcohol, which reaches the stomach blended with food, can already be broken down and "detoxified" in the stomach.

A U.S. study has shown that wine consumption during

mealtimes brings other health benefits. Of 15,000 subjects, those who took their wine between meals were in general more susceptible to various pathogens and displayed a four times greater overall mortality than the more disciplined group in the study.

One need only look at the classic wine regions around the Mediterranean to realize that higher than average wine consumption does not necessarily equal excessive consumption. In Mediterranean countries, wine is not a mere luxury or indulgence; it is a standard component in nutrition. It is a normal part of everyone's daily diet, just like bread and water. Enjoying wine is firmly integrated into daily family rituals, such as mealtimes, and this keeps consumption under control and also plays an important role in shaping the attitude of young people towards drinking wine. In contrast to other European and North American countries, where young people "hit the bottle" in search of euphoria, intoxication or an elusive feeling of happiness, the youth in France or Italy tend to develop a much more balanced and mature attitude towards alcoholic beverages, which helps to protect them against alcohol abuse in adulthood.

...but with Regularity

Throughout this book the point has been made repeatedly that red wine's benefits for the heart are closely linked to regular, that is to say daily, consumption. The reason is that both alcohol and the phenol compounds—in other words, the two components relevant to cardiac health—act only for short periods of time before being metabolized and excreted. This is especially true of the valuable flavonoids (antioxidants) contained in red wine, which

The recommendation to drink wine moderately and regularly is based upon the fact that the valuable wine flavonoids are active in the bloodstream only for a relatively short time.

seem to become inactive very rapidly. To supply the body with sufficient amounts of these materials, it is therefore necessary to ingest them regularly.

Anyone who believes that the recommended weekly intake could all be consumed in a great binge on the weekend with similar beneficial results would be terribly wrong: such extreme fluctuations are of no benefit to the heart, and the sudden oxidating stress could seriously damage the liver. By contrast, regular and moderate consumption of red wine presents no risk to the liver whatsoever, since it is easily capable of quickly detoxifying small amounts of alcohol. Only when such moderate amounts are exceeded and the liver cannot keep up does it have to search for an alternative route, so to speak, by metabolizing the alcohol. This is invariably accompanied by an increased production of free radicals, which damage the organ in the long term. (The significance and danger of oxidation are described on page 66.)

More Protection during the High-Risk Years

For men, the risk of damage or disease in the coronary vessels usually begins at the age of thirty. Cholesterol levels gradually increase between the ages of thirty and fifty-five. Since a high cholesterol level is among the main risk factors for arteriosclerosis, these are the years when the greatest amount of damage is done to the coronary vessels, even if it goes undetected. Therefore, men should pay particular attention to their diet during this period of their life and ensure that they receive a sufficient supply of antioxidants.

In women, the risk of cholesterol deposits in the vessels increases with the hormonal changes that accompany menopause.

Variety is the Best Strategy

You don't need to be a connoisseur to know that great differences exist among red wines. There is a wide variety of flavors, for example, and, as we now recognize, varying levels of flavonoid concentration. Since flavonoids are the basis for the "wine miracle" in their role as antioxidants, scientists have naturally tried to determine which wines are particularly high in these valuable components. Unfortunately, the findings have been disappointing. While it was determined that certain wines are very high in the flavonoid resveratrol (see page 69), the same wines were found to be very low in quercetin (see page 71).

Since no conclusive evidence exists at this time as to which flavonoid is most beneficial to the heart, it would make little sense to base a recommendation on these findings. Moreover, different vintages of one and the same wine have revealed a range of flavonoid concentrations. All this offers little help in deciding for or against any particular wine.

Because of the difficulties involved in naming the "ultimate" wines for cardiac health benefits, nutritionists recommend that one should avoid limiting your selection to any particular type of wine or vintage. Experts feel that the best approach is to sample as many wines as possible, choosing the one that is best for each given meal. And this would seem to agree with common sense, for surely wine should remain a pleasure and not become a boring, unvarying component of a health regime.

There is no specific wine for heart protection. The best recommendation is to try as great a variety as possible.

Support your heart by avoiding risk factors for the cardiovascular system. At the very top of the list: quit smoking!

Other Healthy Habits for Your Heart

Moderate consumption of red wine is undoubtedly an effective method of lowering the risk of coronary heart disease and heart attack. However, there are other good means of promoting a healthy heart. One is to avoid the known risk factors for arteriosclerosis (see page 27). Among these factors it is important to mention tobacco, which narrows the blood vessels (increasing blood pressure) and also releases a chain reaction of free radicals in the body.

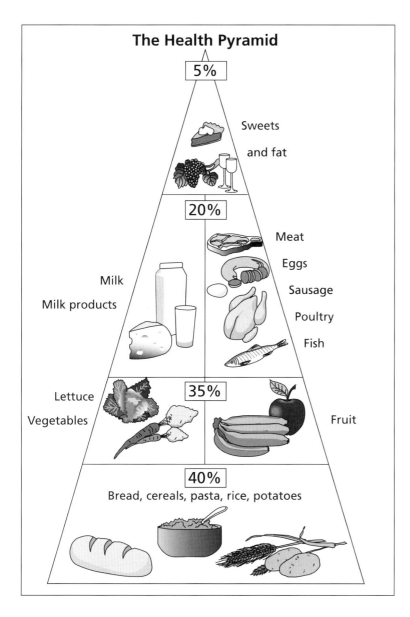

The Health Pyramid

5%

Sweets
and fat

20%

Meat

Eggs

Sausage

Poultry

Fish

Milk
Milk products

35%

Lettuce
Vegetables

Fruit

40%

Bread, cereals, pasta, rice, potatoes

The "health pyramid" symbolizes the relative importance of different food groups in one's daily diet. The most important group includes bread, cereals, etc. (40 percent). Sweets and fat should not compose more than 5 percent of one's daily diet.

Good Health through Exercise

Another major risk factor for heart attack is inadequate exercise, a common feature of Western societies. The fact that intensive physical activity plays an important role in cardiac health can be seen simply by looking at the statistics, which show that people who avoid strenuous physical activity throughout their lives run twice or even three times the risk of heart attack compared with others.

Regular exercise (but not weight or resistance training) ensures that blood pressure is maintained at a healthy level and that the metabolism is regulated by increasing the "good" HDL cholesterol. Exercise also decreases the risk of clotting and prevents weight gain, which is a risk factor in a number of diseases. In this way, regular exercise provides both direct and indirect action against heart attack and stroke; and the more risk factors are present, the greater the benefits of regular exercise.

A note of caution, however: avoid over-exercising! Physical activity should create balance and satisfaction, not pain and stress. Only if you feel well in whatever training you undertake will you decrease stress hormones and counteract unhealthy irritants—both of which are important triggers for cardiovascular disease.

Nutrition—The Mediterranean Model

The link between poor diet and damaged blood vessels has been known for some time and has formed the subject of many studies. In the framework of this book we shall therefore restrict our comments to providing a general overview of the most important nutritional rules. The general recommendation today is for a diet high in grain products and fresh fruit and vegetables, but low in animal protein and fat. Nutritionists praise the traditional Mediterranean kitchen as a model for a healthy diet. The cuisine of the Mediterranean, in combination with red wine consumption, is the most likely reason why the people in these regions have such positive statistics for cardiac health.

Using the Mediterranean food culture (which is predominantly vegetarian) as a model, the following guidelines have been established for healthy nutrition:

• Our daily diet should be based on grains and cereals. This means that bread, pasta, rice or cereals should form a part of every meal. Potatoes too should have a fixed place on the menu.

• Fruit and vegetables should compose a good third of the daily calorie intake, with vegetables slightly more dominant than fruit. We can eat up to 2.2 pounds (1 kg) of vegetables per day and three servings of fruit. Fresh fruit and vegetables are rich in vitamins and antioxidants, which are used by the body to combat aggressive free radicals.

• Animal products like milk, cheese, dairy products, eggs, fish, sausage and meat should not exceed one-quarter of the daily food intake. These foods should be avoided above all because animal fat—especially that contained in milk, butter, cheese and eggs—is considered one of the most lethal artery killers when taken in large amounts.

• Sweets are to be avoided, and fats and oils should be used sparingly. Olive oil is recommended for cooking and food preparation instead of butter or margarine. Olive oil is rich in unsaturated fat, which helps to regulate cholesterol levels by increasing the "good" HDL cholesterol, and is also a good source of vitamin E, which prevents arteriosclerosis.

The Mediterranean Diet and Heart Attacks

A French study delivered impressive proof of the preventive effect of the Mediterranean diet on heart attacks. Six hundred heart attack patients were given either the standard low-fat diet usually prescribed for people suffering from heart disease or a diet based on the Mediterranean model (mainly grains and cereals, with lots of vegetables and fish but little beef and pork). The result: the "Mediterranean group" showed a 70 percent lower risk of suffering a second heart attack than the other group. Correspondingly, the mortality rate in the control group was lowered by 70 to 80 percent.

All the Goodness of Wine in a Capsule

Red wine should be drunk first and foremost for its delectable flavor, despite all the health benefits that have been discovered in recent years. If you don't like wine or prefer other alcoholic beverages, or if you want to avoid alcohol altogether for other health reasons, you can still benefit from the "French paradox" without drinking a drop of alcohol or wine. Red wine extracts contain no alcohol but all the healthy ingredients of the beverage. The supplements are available in pharmacies and drugstores under many different brand names, for example VINOPUR® or Sanitas Red Wine Capsules.

> Instead of drinking two glasses of red wine, you could take one red wine capsule as a supplement; the benefit is the same.

An advantage of these supplements over the natural product is that they are standardized; therefore, you can be certain that each capsule contains the same concentration of the effective ingredients. For example, one capsule of VINOPUR contains 40 to 60 mg of polyphenols, which is equivalent to two glasses of red wine.

Thus, red wine extracts enable you to enjoy the same health benefits in a very simple manner, and it's much less expensive than drinking red wine. Still, you won't have the pleasure of tasting a good vintage or any of the other fringe benefits associated with drinking wine.

A Healthy Heart is Not a Matter of Good Luck

As we have seen, cardiac health and performance are strongly linked to lifestyle. Whether we will age with a healthy heart or a damaged one is therefore largely in our own hands. If we avoid unhealthy influences such as stress and cigarettes, pay attention to our diet, exercise regularly and take a glass of red wine with our meals, we create the best conditions for long-lasting cardiac health.

> **The best heart protection is a good lifestyle. Daily, moderate wine consumption is only one component.**

Index